After th

ROBERT MINHINNICK was born in   ...I
Wales. He works for the environmen   ...es and is
also a freelance writer and editor. His   ...ie Cholmondeley
Award and the Forward Prize for Best   ...ual Poem, 1999. His first
book of essays, *Watching the Fire Eater* (Seren) was Welsh Book of the Year
in 1993. He edits the quarterly magazine, *Poetry Wales*.

Also by Robert Minhinnick from Carcanet

Selected Poems

ROBERT MINHINNICK

After the Hurricane

CARCANET

Acknowledgements

Some of these poems have appeared in *Twentieth-Century Poetry in English*, ed. Michael Schmidt; *Twentieth-Century Anglo Welsh Poetry*, ed. Dannie Abse; the *Forward Books of Poetry*, 2000 and 2001; *Literary Review* (USA); *New Welsh Review*; *PN Review*; *Pivot* (USA); *Planet*; *Poetry London*; *Poetry Wales*; *Red Poets Society*; *Scintilla*; *Wading Through Deep Water – The Parkinson's Anthology*, ed. Tony Curtis.

First published in Great Britain in 2002 by
Carcanet Press Limited
4th Floor, Conavon Court
12–16 Blackfriars Street
Manchester M3 5BQ

A CIP catalogue record for this book
is available from the British Library
ISBN 1 85754 563 X

The publisher acknowledges financial assistance
from the Arts Council of England

Set in Monotype Ehrhardt by XL Publishing Services, Tiverton
Printed and bound in England by SRP Ltd, Exeter

Contents

Twenty-Five Laments for Iraq

The muezzin voices break the night
Telling us of what we are composed:
Coffee grits; a transparency of sugar;
The ghost of the cardamom in the cup's mosque.

*

These soldiers will not marry.
They are betrothed already
To the daughters of uranium.

*

Scheherazade sits
In heat and dust
Watching her bucket fill.
This is the first story.

*

Before hunger
        Thirst.
Before prayer
        Thirst.
Before money
        Thirst.
Before Thirst
        Water.

*

Boys of Watts and Jones County
Build cookfires on the ramparts of Ur.
But the desert birds are silent
And all the wolves of the province
Fled to the north.

*

While we are filming the sick child
The sick child behind us
Dies. And as we turn our camera
The family group smartens itself
As if grieving might offend.

*

Red and gold
The baldaquins
Beneath the Baghdad moon,
Beneath the Pepsi globe.

*

Since the first Caliph
There has been the suq –
These lemons, this fish:
And hunched over the stone
The women in their black –
Four dusty aubergines.

*

My daughter, he says,
Stroking the Sony DV cam,
Its batteries hot, the tally light red.
My daughter.

But his daughter, 12, keeps to her cot,
Woo, woo, wooing like the hoopoe
Over the British Cemetery.

*

What are children here
But olive stones under our shoes?
Reach instead for the date
Before its brilliance tarnishes.

*

Back and forth
Back and forth
The Euphrates kingfisher,
The ferryman's rope.

*

The ice-seller waits
Beneath his thatch of palm,
His money running in the gutter's tilth.

*

Over the searchlights
And machine-gun nests on Rashid Street
The bats explode like tracer fire.

*

Yellow as dates these lizards
Bask on the basilica.
Our cameraman removes his shoes,
Squats down to pray.

*

Radiant,
With the throat of a shark,
The angel who came to the hundreds
Sheltered in Amiriya.

*

In the hotel carpark
One hundred and fifty brides and grooms
Await the photographer.
All night I lie awake
Listening to their cries.

*

This first dollar peeled off the wad
Buys a stack of dinars higher than my heart.

*

A heron in white
And a woman in black
Knee-deep together
In the green Tigris.

*

Her two pomegranates lie beside the bed
But they have carried the child away.

*

She alights from the bus
In a cloud of black,
The moon and stars upon her skirt,
And painted across her breast
The Eye that Sees All Things.

*

The vermilion on his toenails
   Is almost worn away,
This child of the bazaar,
Who rolls my banknote to a tube
And scans through its telescope
The ruins of Babylon.

*

Four billion years
Until the uranium
That was spilled at Ur
Unmakes itself.
Easier to wait for the sun to die.

*

In the Ministry of Information
Computers are down, the offices dark;
But with me in the corridor
A secret police of cockroaches.

*

Moths, I say.
No. Look again, she suggests.
Fused to the ceiling are the black hands
Of the children of Amiriya.

*

Sometimes
The certainties return:
These cushions, a pipe,
And the sweet Basran tea
Stewed with limes.

The Bombing of Baghdad as seen from an Electrical Goods Shop

Eating was serious work.
I watched you arrange as an evening ritual
The hummus rough with lemonrind
And bread dusted with Jordanian thyme.

Every supper, you said, might be the last.
So maybe that's the way to live,
The way that we should read our books
Or view as now at home this notch of sea
Silvered and thunderstruck
Between the pillars of the esp,
A ladle of spelter hissing at the air.

Nazaar, I know the market place today
Must be quiet as the British Cemetery,
That field with headstones of forgotten boys
Who died of cholera and Baghdad heat.

There's no haggling with the smoke-seller
Or the women with switchsticks, flicking
Flies away from Tigris bream:
The honey and grapes and Syrian soap
Are stalled in convoys along the border road.

And I suppose that you're at home,
Because where else is there to be on a night like this,
Listening to the Cruise missiles, the only
Traffic out tonight on Palestine Street,
While here in the window of Edwards Electrical
Your city in the tracers' glow
Becomes a negative of itself.

The Discovery of Radioactivity

When Monsieur Bequerel returns to Paris
He takes out a key and unlocks a drawer
In his desk. Then he understands.

It is as if the black stone he had placed there
Is breathing. Something has come out of it.
The hot soul of the stone squats in the dark of the desk.

One hundred years later
I edge the Astro as far as the barbed wire:
The road ends with a warning sign

With the warning worn away.
In the prickly pear our geiger starts to percolate.
It is as if somewhere the junco, somewhere the chickadee

Were scolding us. But Daniel speaks
Our instructions. Stay here too long
And we'll give the daughters of uranium

A bedroom in our bones.
So no one lives here now.
No one will ever live here

But the desert poltergeists –
Thorium, Americium, each a wild child
Run off into the world,

Performing great deeds, performing terrible deeds,
But beyond us now, strayed forever out of reach.
Ah, Monsieur Bequerel, help us to understand.

When our sun is as small as the heart of the prickly pear
The atoms of your black stone
Will still scintillate,

Compulsive as that key you finger
In the pocket of your waistcoat,
Impatient on the journey home.

The Orchids at Cwm y Gaer

Now, disbelieving, I will go
Down a road so narrow
I must travel sideways
Though still the willows will swat me with their swags of rain
And my own sweat tighten under my arms
    As once my father's fingers did.

Step carefully
For here they are,
Newborn but already white with webs.
    Once the superstitious thought
    It was Christ's blood that mottled the leaves,
But now it's as easy to suppose
That these eruptions, under a shadow's anglepoise,
    Are uranium rods
    Broken through from the terrible core.

    We build our legends;
    We build our gods;
But how does a people understand its gods?
    These might be such, thrusting up
Like the pillars of the reactor,
Their alpha-love kissing our skin,
Their gamma-love passing through our bones
To leave their ghosts forever hidden in our chromosomes.

We are people who worships gods
Whose mouths gasp electric,
                      whose eyes
Are a dull, totalitarian
Gold, whose commerce is strange
As a rockpool's
            pornography.

I pause one moment
On this narrow road
With the light tipping out of a tree's tundish
And the spiders at their riot after rain.
Already a thread hangs from my hair
And ties me to this place.
So I open my hands to the orchids at Cwm y Gaer
And count each breath.
How long before the welts appear?
How soon before the cradle of nightsweats,
Or that deep, enriched delirium, dark as dew?

Regulars

Put your foot on the rail; your hands flat
Like a card player who has thrown away.
Then carefully look round.
There are men who are wearing dead men's clothes;
Men who might have been useful
With oxy or a rat-tailed file;
Mad men; madding men; men
Whose tattoos have faded to blue
Inexactitudes on loose muscle;
Men with nicotine eyes;
Men with 43 per cent and rising
Johnnie Walker Black Label complexions;
Men drowning in stonedust
And men with lunar phrenology;
Men with wall-chained Staffordshire
Mastiffs in riveted collars
And brass-studded leather belly-belts;
Solitary men in corners about whom
Plays the violet light of a thunderstorm;
Men in gangs at ease with other men
And the familiar rituals of men; men who carouse
And men who mutter all the shithouse
Salutations known to men;
Men with magnifying glasses
And hollow aluminium walking-frames
On rubber hooves; men
Without teeth and men without stomachs;
Men who stand here for the last time
And men who never stand anywhere else.
Then the landlord slides a drink in front of you:
The beads around the glass are a muck sweat.

Elementary Songs

Hydrogen

Think of a pilot light
Blue as a cornflower,
Then the growl beyond your sleep
As the furnace wakes.

Lithium

Hey man, I'm famous.
That Kurt Cobain wrote a song about me.
And all I ever wanted to do
Was lie here in the tall grass and dream.

Carbon

Murdered, they buried me
With a pestle of wheat, a wineskin.
Now as the ice melts
Whose face is it you recognise
Grinning behind the glacier?

Nitrogen

My wedding dress
Of pearl and aragonite.
See how carefully I step
Before the thrilling train of the air.

Oxygen

I have a gin and orange in The Angel at Rotherhithe
And a snowball in The Mayflower
And listen to the river slapping
Every barge's arse on the way to The Pool.

Sodium

There's not a boy-racer on Wyndham Street
To touch me. You hear that engine revving in the night?
Think of the glow as the petrol tank explodes
At 3 a.m. on the forestry track.

Magnesium

Outcast and amnesiac
I wandered the blacklands
Of Badiet Esh Sham
Until one night in a shepherd's fire
I learned my destiny.

Phosphorus

From the ocean floor
I can still see the moon, my brother:
His eye of dust, the leper's skin;
A lesson to us all, I think.

Sulphur

I am the sunflower
Dishevelled in frost.
Set my tail afire
And watch me skim amongst rooftops,
The bolide that falls
Always beyond the horizon

Chlorine

At last I come upon Port Talbot,
Its sky full of flamingos.
I will enter the citadel from the sea,
My barges filled with sandalwood and saffron.

Calcium

When I dream
There is always that child,
The green star of her fontanelle
Aglow in the dusk,
War and famine
The baubles that fall from her hand.

Iron

Numberless, my children now:
Peachstone, cherrystone,
The jet necklace within the papaya.
Feel how the planet has grown
Succulent around my seed.

Silver

Son of Man
Before man ever was,
From my bivouac
In the cordillera
I send you tributes
Of lilies and icebergs
And an Italian cuirass.
Fashion me songs in return.

Xenon

Virgin of the air,
My sisters offered shelter
On condition I swore the terrible vow.
So how do I know time passes?
By the sharpening of the bones within my skull.

Caesium

Down Babylon's Procession Street
I walked with dragons and eagle-beaked dogs,
And for the first time I knew happiness.
I felt I had come home.

Gold

For your own good
Forget me. All I am
Is an idea under pressure.
What sent Africa
Drifting away like a sailboat
Made me.

Mercury

Attention Deficiency Disorder?
Look, that one trick I sold to Jesus,
He built a whole career out of it.
Think what I could achieve
If I really started to try.

Lead

Remember the day
I caught the lightning bolts?
I planted them here
Where the aconite and the archangel
Are first out of the frost.
What a show they are going to make.

Astatine

A low, anorectical flame
The earth hardly bothered to light.
How close to not existing
Might existence burn?

Osmium

Did you see the fat slob
On the cover of the *National Inquirer* –
The one who couldn't get out of his own front door?
Yeah, it was me.
Why not come over some time,
Tell me how things are going out there.

Francium

The pterodactyl and the cadillac
Are the same to me.
I had vanished from this world
Before thought ever was.
Yet still a place is kept at the banquet.

Radium

Cold runs the current
That carries the golden simulacra of the leaves.
Only children who know how to look
Have ever seen my face.

Uranium

God was ashamed.
He hid his secret
Under the Black Mesa
Until Mr Oppenheimer arrived
And drove me back to the ranch
To freshen up.

Plutonium

Dizzy, I lie
In a darkened room.
From the window I hear
The others calling, but Mama says
I must never go out again.

Californium

Another day, another chatshow.
The tan, the dark glasses,
The half-life of fame.
So who am I then?
Go on, tell me who I am.

Lawrencium

They found me
In the Accelerator Tunnel
At Berkeley, listening
To the song of the calliope.
I counted eight notes flung to heaven
And so learned the purpose of my life.

One Moment on the Avenida

Save us mother.
I saw DNA's double helix
doing the lambada, the girl
from Santa Theresa in the red rubber sheath
– all hips and lips they said –
and her hands restless as mahogany flowers
in the wind that blows out of the backlands
and down the avenida.

Save us, mother,
as the samba reaches to the tropic of capricorn
I never knew existed in my blood,
to the equator that is an iron band around my skull,
save us, for the girl is so close now,
her dance a shimmy
in every shining molecule.

Save us,
for we are the peasants with broken hands;
the worms in our bellies have jewelled mouths,
and we march our milkeyed children
out of the backlands and down the avenida,
pushing over the barracas, stealing Pepsi from the lanchonettes,
because it's the time of the reckoning,
it's the judgement hour
on Ipanema of the dangerous wave.

So mother, save us.
Can you hear us shouting?
Take away, we shout, take away the drought and the chiggers
and the caatinga from our chromosomes.
Make us as rich as the pimps and the moneychangers
on the Avenida Princesa Isabel.

And mother, we will stay
at the Sheraton and feast upon
a river porpoise flown from the market at Belem,
and the army will not move us
nor the thunder in Minas Gerais
nor memoranda from all the laptops in the Centro,
and we will turn on the televisions in the celebrity suites
and the girl in red will dance for us,
the seductress of the genes, she will dance for us, mother.

  And when at last
her spinning has ceased
and we have drunk the gold beer of *Antartica*
in the minibars, she will cry with us,
for she is a peasant girl too,
and she will lead us the long walk home, rejoicing,
    in her red shoes.

Carioca

It's a 127
     Going to the Rodoviaria
And the driver tapping his head.
He's saying I'm loco, I think:
     Loco,
     The locoman,
And as usual there's a crush

So already her breasts
Are pushing into me –
     A gold ring
Between the cups of her bikinitop –
Her face a thin carioca's face
     But the body
     An oiled cuirass;

     And the bus is bucking
Among the taxis on Avenida Atlantica
And outside the children of the traffic islands and tunnelmouths
Are sharing bags of manioc and beans,
Sucking fishbones thrown from the lanchonettes
     And the driver is pulling
     At his eyelid,

     Look, lookman
And at last I understand,
     But her hands are so swift
I cannot feel
The razor slitting the bagstraps
     Or the velcro
     Opening its cat's mouth,

But my hands are against her breasts now,
     Beautiful travesties
               Silver as phosphorus
     And her eyes a centimetre away
Irreducible shots of the barraca's
     Aguardente –
Those first sips

That lighten the head
And stiffen the knee –
And her smell a mansmell because I know that smell
 Then somehow she is through the turnstile
        And I am shivering
Like a hummingbird shivers
        Over its own image.

Questions of The Woman Who Fell

Ah the sea,
Its screed adazzle.
How many like you
Have failed its puzzle?

I find the ledge you must have climbed
And lord it over thirty miles,
Each footstep munching corals in the chalk.
But why choose this place when you need to talk?

Nameless now
       You have become
The woman who fell:
Or rather
       The Woman Who Fell
Still clutching her mobile phone.
So what was the story you were planning to tell?

Did you hear the linnet
– Little geisha of the gorse –
Its three notes dialling 999?
But you had found a better benzodiazepine.

Below you spread
The hermaphroditic world.
Had you then, lady,
Run out of people to be?

Purpleblack and green as figs
The sea-lace spreads across the rocks.
Mark how it tethers
Itself in all weathers:
Why was it then that you let go
So easily of all we know?

Had you considered the fair
And its timetabled mania?
At night I have seen the wheels'
Last circuits above the town:
Gold and fast then faster and more golden
With every revolution.
                    How they fix
The eye with their pyrotechnics.
If you had watched those lights upon the sea
Would you have felt a part of the pageantry?

        Hellenic
        Ovenstick
    And an aerosol from Japan.
We have to learn the tide's lesson:
        Avoid the literal.
        Live the littoral.

It was never the rockrose
Indomitable in the grykes
That led you here, or a sweep of the sea
On the last day of the August weeks
It would look like that:
A stannary's whiteblue.
What else was overwhelming but the view?

In the cave behind the rock pools
    My torchlight has revealed
Fossils crouched as though in prayer
    To the gods of limestone
A listener will hear laughing in these cliffs.
But who teaches us to read such hieroglyphs?

Wand erect,
        Mast on the hill,
But did numbers prove
        Of use at all?
We live in language,
        That limestone fault
Between sweetwater
        And mortifying salt.

From the giant screen, the voice of Cher
Behind her laminarian hair
Sang *Do you believe?*
                    Do you believe
In love ever after?
Lady, you were unimpressed
By that exquisite evangelist.
But why so quick to quit the fair
And take the hard road of thin air?

These molluscs might
Be shoemaker's knives:
   How deadly are
Such brainless lives?
And think of the sea-hare
   Grazing the tide;
What kind of a creature
Carries its shell *inside*?

A good place for the drift-pickers:
   You would have seen that log
      Of mahogany
Months out of Maranhao
Or the Ihla de Marajo,
      Roseblack totem
         On the sand of Gwter Hopsog.
It's chainsawn to a stump by now,
Hauled off to backyard joinerys.
Curious what's found floating in these seas.

So listen, lady,
The sea's a cinema,
A multiscreen alhambra.
Had you never heard Liz Taylor
Calling to you on salt-laden air,
Or Burton's baritoning of despair
Within the waves' polyphony?
It might break our hearts
But it's their performance. We're still working on our parts.

Parachutes of jellyfish
Had blown in from the warm Atlantic.
Did you watch the ocean blossom with their silk?

No use black polish
    And the shining-brush?
The salt insists
In silver fingerprints,
As if the sea was somehow holding on.
Or you'd kicked a hole in the white horizon.

    Your phone rang
At sunset. And there was Venus,
All horns and teeth.
Everything was fine, you said.
Below you the ocean
Was pacing its chamber.
I'd wage the last face you remember
Was your own.

You fell into the chaos of the karst –
    Three hundred million years
    In three seconds
To break upon lime-lilies,
Those bones of flowers that built our tropical coasts.
But tell me what island isn't full of ghosts?

In mid-air had it sunk in
Impatience is a deadly sin?
To learn there is no late and soon
You should have studied this lagoon:
    Which is where they found your phone,
    Still charged, the numbers racing
    Over its square of sky.
Goodbye,
    goodbye,
        goodbye,
            goodbye,
Goodbye?

Misadventure makes no sense.
Instead I choose the wave's verdict
That everything will be returned
Though it comes unrecognised.
    But the ocean laughs;
    It splits its sides.
    Your name's rubbed smooth
    Within the book of tides.

Samphire

After the hurricane blew
Through my head I knew

Things had to change. That silence
Was no longer a defence.

So walking on the eastern shore
I asked myself what I was for,

And on that beach I built a fire
For the pickers of samphire,

Their plasticbags and fingers thick
With the samphire's citric

Oils, our thoughts turning to supper
Of seabass, or a silver-

Side of sewin laid
In tinfoil in the pit I'd made

On a griddle over ingots
Of driftwood, white-hot

In seconds, the firestones black
With armfuls of the bladderwrack

Like strings of jalapenos spread
To dry, so that the fire spat

Purple as tramsparks, its smoke a sail
To the northeast, and as night fell

We saw spectres in that auditorium,
Our shadows in the salty flame –

Giants as the blaze grew higher
Crowned with pluckings of samphire –

And then behind us on the dune
Another light appeared, and soon

Another, further up the bay,
And voices if we listened carefully,

Some soft, some crazed
In the darkness where the fires blazed,

White lightning drinkers
Under the flickering meniscus

Of the dogstar, and speedfreaks'
Midnight histrionics,

Mad as sandfleas round the beacon
On the summit of Tom Brython,

Ambassadors of turbulence
Whose private language yet made sense,

Then deep in the dewpits of the warren
The nightjar's prothalamium

To a new moon: true voices all
In the dark's confessional,

Admitting the imperative
That how we speak is how we live,

And even our deliriums
Are more than débris of our dreams.

So when I heard the hurricane
I guessed it might not come again,

But what it offers is the choice
To use, or not, a tiny voice

And watch it flaring like a spark
In duneland's neolithic dark.

And maybe the next morning find
The fire has left a frost behind.

Songs for the Lugmen

1

Weeks
Of high pressure.
Even the earth is foreign.
But in these caves I discover
The sigh of the subterranean...

Then, on the Weather Channel
A swell off the Azores.
And we feel it.
          We feel it.
The Gulf Stream in us roars.

2

Two lovers lie beneath the stack:
Wiggling like wheatears,
   their arses white
Against the rock wall's black.

And the lugmen laugh
And come down the sandy trail,
The tyres of their bicycle
Hissing, the young one looking back.

3

In the dunes, nothing grows taller
   than a man's arms aloft.
Our desert is a golden tarp
         thrown over limestone.
More memory there than Microsoft.

Around us this pampas
Of viper and thorn,
   the cinnabar moon
Grinning like a computer virus.

The lugmen have taken off their shirts.
How pale they are;
                       and faded their tattoos.
The older cycles through the surf,
Handlebars hung with shoes.

And I come later, wandering
The long line of their pits,
Each with its hillock
                       of nickel-coloured sand
Where the sea circulates.

5

Ah, I have tried to comprehend
    the orchids' telepathy.
But their thoughts are lightning bolts
    earthed too deep for me.

Yet in these caves I overhear
    the gods of limestone whisper
Before the sea begins its climb
    like a shining escalator.

6

The younger lies upon his side
With his arm thrust in the sand.
Now there is a serpent, blind
And silver, wrapped around his hand.

The old man waits, holding the pail.
Lug are lug; he knows their ways:
Even the big villains, dug from their crypt,
Can no longer amaze.

7

How far down is out of reach?
                Li-lo,
        marlinspike,
Drowned abbot's crozier
Are sunk together at the roots of the beach.

So the lugmen smoke and dig again,
Oblivious to the bathers,
The mothers and children sat in the surf,
The solitary fathers.

8

The future lies beneath their feet,
Laid out in this savannah
Where the coming and the going meet
And transform one another.

The lugmen on their knees
Are listening at the pools.
In their bucket I see vitriols;
Lenses that look through geologies.

9

There they crouch into the breeze, mouths pursed like anemones.
Salt and samphire on the tongue
But how briefly lasts the lozenge
Of language.

They seek no scenery.
Only the pools of Ffynnon Wen
Where the thief and the murderer
Are baptised again
                and again.

10

Above us is the thunderhead
And suddenly a sky
Pulling itself inside out.
The crowds have turned away.

So who knows what the lugmen know
Or if what they know contains
The beginning of weather,
                         the ending of weather
In Africa's red rains.

Lac la Ronge

I dream
Of a lake that is endless.
Of a lake
That is a white mind.

Outside this window
In the dark where all I see
Are the lights of the snowcats
Like fireflies in the muskeg,
The Cree children are moving in drunken circles
(A little gas
             goes a long way)

Over the drive-in diner of the ice
The football field of the ice
The astroturf of the ice
The nature reserve of the ice
The supermarket parkade of the ice
The hunting lodge the school the radio station
The casino the beverage-room the reservation
Of the ice.

            I dream
Of a lake that is endless.
That serves for a world.

This is hard for me.
I come from a place
Where life is fertilised by salt
And at 8 a.m. every morning
The isopods leave their labyrinths of stone,
Strong armed in motorcycle leathers,
And muscle down the boulevards shouting
Out of the way, out of the way,
Where scorpion fish crouch sullen as flints
At the tide's interchange,
                          and the sea
Departs and arrives on its grey commute,
Where surfers cry out as the horizon travels
In the wrong direction over their heads,

And ghosthour begins,
Ghost-hour,
      ghost
          hour
When the invisibles walk the esplanade
And the salt inside us
Calls back to the ocean,
The riptide of the blood.

 Now there's a raven on my wheelie bin
   – ruffian in a long black coat –
And boys in Chevrolets with green provincial plates
 – The poorer the town
               the bigger the car –
Those shock-shot lowriders
With melt up to the doors
And laughing sisters in the trunk
Gone down Hastings Street on the way to Orange Julius.

      Soon
They will dig
For Thiessen's,
      live in a dormitory
In the no-go zone,
Bulldoze waste into drumlins,
And play video poker under the uranium moon.
But their home will be
      the lake.

Now the La Ronge ghosts conspire,
   apply their lipsalve,
     dance in the shower,
       scroll channels with the remote.

I stand under the tamarack
And listen to their whispering
In a language that has no alphabet:
A speech my other world thinks is extinct.

A glacier
Large as a European country
Dug the lake out of the shield:
A chevron in granite
Still
      chill
   in the night
Though the melt runs all day
And already the new mosquitos
   – *Lullay lullay* on barbed wire –
Besiege the air.

Beneath the lake is a basement room
With the furnace turned down low
And a family around a dead TV.
   Above their heads is a single star
That transfixes them:
   Venus,
         like the eye
Of a wolverine.

     I dream
Of a lake that is endless.
     Of a lake
That is a white mind.

At dawn I part the motel blind
And there is the raven again
Or maybe a man on the shore
   in a long black coat:

In one hand he holds thunder
   and with the other
A tantalus of lightning
Scarlet as a Saskatchewan lily.

Ah, La Ronge beneath its ice:
   a sun eclipsed.
I might walk across its miles
And still not think that it was real:

Or take the snowcat and burn
        my name into its face
And yet write
Nothing on nothing.

I dream of a lake
Like a white mind.
        Ah La Ronge,
Where the shoals flick and weave

Glittering like firebrats
Under the masonry of ice.
        Where the bald eagle
Is stretched across the saloon bar —

A judge whose silver horsehair hangs awry
        as he hears each alibi.
Where salmon pucker like Sunday aunts
Against the trophy glass.

La Ronge, La Ronge,
        further than Thule:
And a thousand lakes beyond the horizon
That the world is still to name.

Coyotes

The thaw brings smartweed, cockleburr,
The shearing man your parents used.
And with it comes that prophesy

Of what we know will happen
No matter how we turn in our beds
Or kill channel after channel with the remote.

In the wood we found the hawk's platform,
Snow still cupped in a breast-rounded chamber:
And then you pointed out the den.

Coyotes, sons of bitches, you said,
Tongues red as the dogwood,
Eyes you should never look into:

They would screw the farmdogs, kill the birds.
So you will leave the dead lamb where
They can drag it under the electric fence.

Tonight within the farmhouse light
We listen for sheep, first time back in the pasture,
The ice-groans from the lake:

But neither flock nor cold speaks what we hear.
Evening time means all we need
Is a place to hang a slicker; a good sipping whisky.

Yet now you say
We have to do this:
Not every year but now it must be done.

You put on gloves
And work the poison
Into the carcass of the lamb,

Seeding the flesh, anointing the heart
And liver, already greening, mineral,
Its fleece a sleeve turned outside in.

Back in town I have a glass table
Dirty with words, a hearthstone
Where a fossil creature shines.

On Temperance Street my neighbours
Face down the cold in their determined clothes:
But here the town has never been.

So the pellets pass out of your hands
In wisdom, science, small despair:
They are the brand your father used.

The thaw brings smartweed, cockleburr,
The prairie crocus, blotting-paper blue.
Out in the dark the coyotes start their chant.

A Natural History of Saskatchewan

Porcupine

What's black and white
And dead all over?

Just enough traffic on this highway
To ensure you never made it back

To the sett beyond the slough.
But close up, you don't make sense.

Down on my knees I discover
A baby smiling under a warbonnet.

Nodding Donkeys

All day the drill-rigs genuflect
To the gods of distances;

And at night on the plain
We hear their pistons sigh

As they penetrate the ore of frost.
Look, dawn brings a stain

Seeping through the prairie earth.
Oil is their clover opening to the sun.

Moose

Here stands old swampbreath
Raggeder than the muskeg –
Nosedown in a wheelie-bin,
Arsebone to the Northern Lights.

Wolverine

Such a cry.
It has torn your own throat.

How the sidebusters cowered
In their stiff clothes,

The rumour of your fury
Grown to a waking dream.

Ah, but they were resolute.
So here you pose

As a beverage-room trophy,
Eyes above the forty ounce Jim Beam,

Feet still raised to make that leap
Back over the tree line.

Firebrat

A nail
Unhammers itself
From the floorboard.

Looks, little sister, like it's you and me.
All the snowbirds have packed
And gone to California.

Outside, if I crossed the avenue,
My breath would fall around my feet
In a muffler of blue ash.

Instead, I watch you,
Turbo-racer from the Cambrian age
In the basement's infra-red,

While the rest of the world
Hunkers down for the dark time.
We're the only ones hereabouts now, sister:

The only ones left.

Pelicans

Where the river bends
A family is squabbling
Over who gets to use the camcorder.

They agree one thing. Nothing's ever right:
Water too cold, the spring come late,
Pickerel devious as mercury.

Tomorrow they'll pack
And find a new campsite.
Listen. The rushes fill with mutterment.

Buffalo Wings

The panic so great behind
That there's no turning back at the cliff-face.

The hunters with their brands and waving arms
Watch your discovery of the air —

That malicious element you never suspected
Lay beyond a world of snow, sweetgrass and snow.

And there you soar, ascending beyond history,
Gone like the smoke-rings from the caboose.

Jay

Down in the badlands
I watch earth blow away.
From the rock it drifts lighter than thistledown.

These cliffs are a dangerous
Music filling my head.
So you are good to hear, good to hear,

Little blue wiseguy
With the carney voice,
Breaking hearts with your

Main Street finery,
Flashing those big gold rings
In your eyes.

Spider

Gone six months, I waited for you
In all the trysting places.

And suddenly here you are
On a bush of silver tundishes,

Every leaf devoured, and your children
Running wild in the road.

Bear

Heading north I met a bear,
Melancholy truant at the edge of the wood.

The bear picked up a stone,
Then replaced it like the lid on a pan.

Nothing there, said its sad snout.
So I looked at the bear and the bear looked at me

At the edge of the tamarack
Where the six months snow had made its last redoubt,

And silence was a language we could share.
And when the bear looked at me and I looked at the bear

I saw the only colour in our world
Was the red tag on its ear

That held the microchip.
In their office the rangers watched

A constellation of bears moving through the map of the park,
As emerging from the slumber

Of their wickiups
The bears rolled their eyes at the world,

Unzipped their tongues
And lifted stones like great thermometers,

And I stood here and the bear stood there,
Moving from foot to foot together in the cold.

Roadkill Blues

Forty years might be a long time to wait
But I won't complain. Your italics
Are unmistakeable, and if I was allowed

One last act in the world, knifing this letter
Would be Top Ten, easy. You ask how it goes,
Iridium across paper fine as peachskin,

And what's to say, but as with forty years,
It goes, it goes. Okay, some days are better
Than others, but nothing so broke it won't fix.

And I'm earning, you know, filthy *arian*.
Got to schmooze for it, which doesn't make me proud,
But there was nothing else on. I better begin.

Tomorrow the museum of barbed wire,
The depression in the plain where the last
Ghost dancer lay down in the prairie sage:

Tomorrow the amphetamine brilliance
Of the sky. But life goes on today.
So I take my hand out of its quilted glove

And wait for the cold, its moment's delay
Only an echo of the light, to sheath
The finger–joints – each nail like a nun's face –

And the blunt, recalcitrant thumb,
In invisible frost. And now I dare myself,
Like the kids who lick the metal posts, and step

Back, leaving a sac of skin, clearer than breath,
To hold the handle of the shopping cart
Fetched out of the deserted parking-lot,

A Safeways trolley, its spokes the fire
Of a brazier. I touch it for you,
There, and am back outside a painted barn

In a field that stretches all the way
To Manitoba, breathing the sweet
Effluvia of the grain elevator,

And watch again the secretary boys
Grab lunch under the statue of Columbus
In Syracuse: Polish sausage, coffees

With lids. Then a walk through the woods
In the Iroquois starlight, the garter
Snakes folded like mittens in the rotten trees,

To hug Annie Dillard goodbye in her dark
Library, that blonde fringe I loved
Hanging over my arm like a winecloth.

Now Carrie, I think that's what her ID says,
Comes back with a refill of the sour
Colombian. It's a quiet night.

Apart from the girls upping the body
Count on a Maximum Karnage video,
I'm the only one in, framed in a window

Big as a cinema screen, while over
On the strip in the plutonian cold
Wendy's offers its combos, and the Venice

House is wrapped in neon vines. And you ask
About the weather. I see it as a friend
Bringing me news, an intelligent friend

With an agenda. The car doors crack like
Pistolshots; while river ice opposite
The Bessborough Hotel has grown thicker

Than a foundation stone. Couples hire skates
From the cloakroom, twist on its glass granite
In the headlights of their Neons, the spray

Flying like spume off a pitcher. But that's
Downtown. I'm out east in suburbia
Where the serial killers play Dire Straits,

Half way between the malls at Circle Park
And Wildwood. They put me in a dream home
But can I ever sleep? By now perhaps

I should have come to terms with its good taste,
The closet mirrors, frames of cedar grain,
Those children who smile behind hornrims

On the corridor wall's collage of snaps,
Blond Dutch in their 'seventies' wide lapels
And graduation gowns, the boy's pale hair

Thinning badly even then, the girl dumbstruck,
But unaware, standing on her wedding train.
I'm saving air-miles for the older son:

Spend more, fly further, it's his kind of deal.
Good people but unrelaxed. They seem to feel
My kitchen style verges on the obscene:

Tomato seeds, Moosehead, rock'n'roll,
So I promise to vinegar their glass
And keep dental floss out of the toilet bowl.

I call their house the Empire of Clean,
Squidging up my cornchip-dust, the Häagan-Dazs.
Dad was in the Credit Union. He ensured

I paid the rent in nine post-dated cheques.
Mom has a chest murmur that means her cheeks
Are aubergine. They're escaping the cold

In a San Diego trailer-park,
And watching their silver convertible
In case the Tijuana kids try again

To reduce it to constituent parts.
Crime troubles them like an allergy;
The murders in the papers chill their hearts.

Before they left they lived in the basement –
Big enough, but lit like a sickroom,
And I would hear the bell of their microwave

Announce each meal time: oddly comforting,
(How simple are the things that make us brave).
But when they left it was the other sounds –

Like freezer-growl or the alien purr
Of the humidifier, somewhere
I cannot locate, that started to annoy.

Wildwood is a lawn-sprinkler, basketball-ring
Kind of place. I overdose on caffeine here
And after months have come to understand

That it needs a careful eye to notice how
A mall changes. Take Ethan. He vanished
Weeks ago from his job as a rose-boy

At the Gourmet Boutique. He would stand
Out on the sidewalk, one day in a midnight-
Blue, the next in a silver tuxedo

With a tray of scarlet rosebuds, each tight
As a pursemouth, wait there lean, impeccable,
Like some shaved marine at Arlington

And dare you to show how cheap you were
By driving past. The suits were on hire
From Evenings Deluxe, also at the mall,

And I admit I miss his self-aimed jokes
In that wry, smalltown Saskatchewan drawl
That meant 'this sucks, but in the meantime, folks',

The perfect bloom he pinned to his lapel.
Ethan was the name of the character
That John Wayne played in *The Searchers*,

To some the greatest Western ever made:
So all these provinces have known Ethans
Ever since. He said his best time came when

A man stepped out of a Cutlass Supreme
And peeled off two hundred for the whole display –
Not bad for a pitch out on the parkade.

So I drink to Ethan and his next grand scheme
And John Wayne's exhausted monomania.
Yet every hour there's a different hero here.

Today mine are: the professor who dug
A whole tyrannosaur out of the badlands
And brought big daddy back to the campus,

Its tiny forearms, thalidomide-shrunk,
Reaching to touch those on the second floor,
A mouth wider than a Cadillac trunk.

And Richard Manuel, feeling music fail,
The rooms of his house furnished with thousands
Of empty Grand Marnier bottles, a drunk

Who died sober in a Florida motel
Hanging by his belt from the shower rail.
Those are the people who leave their spell

Behind, testament to the rest of us
Who never understood what life is for.
You ask if I get lonely. Hard to tell.

But it's only last weekend that I was asked
To a get-together of the exiled Brits:
Tyneside machinists, that couple from Neath,

In a stew of accents that might make
You wince or misty-eyed. Yet it's not too long
Before you know they're all a load of shits,

Goggling about house prices, the rifle club.
During our meal the conversation died
So I thought about the sunflower

That hung above my fence all October,
Its face an emerald paunch of seeds,
An exotic that the cold daily reduced

To a strange reverse image of itself,
The yellow hair fallen in a frost-burnt wreath:
Miss Haversham instead of the new bride.

But that's indoors where the temptation is
To reach for fifths of rye and end up juiced.
Before the cold I spent most afternoons

Looking into the sky from the turnpikes.
Driving to Elbow for time at the beach
I saw a porcupine, first of the roadkills,

Its ruff of needles like an Elizabethan fan.
The Ranchero tyre had broken its back
And it lay with feet extended like a child's

From a swing, the wheatfield almost in reach.
So I gathered up a bouquet of its quills.
Why not? The ants were coming, the loud racoons,

And we kept on south to the Vermillion Hills.
But after that I couldn't stop looking;
It's what drivers here call the roadkill blues,

An inventory that lengthened in my mind
Every time I was invited for a cruise.
One morning in the sanctifying light

I saw someone hit a chickenhawk
On Highway Eleven. You pass them sitting
On fenceposts, eyes full of dismal patience,

Feet like clawhammers. It was as if
A pillow exploded, all those feathers
Like pissed-on snow smeared over red gravel,

And a stain on the fender of that white
Chevrolet Corsica, a woman
In barettes at the wheel, open-mouthed.

Driving's a problem but it's the only way
To learn. I mean *learn*. It's how cowboys travel,
The fourteen-year-olds going to bush parties.

We turned off the highway on a dirt road
To Smuts, where the artists had lived before
The bikers arrived, painting ruined barns

And sunsets. There's nothing left but the church,
Its dome flashing the language of mirrors
And a figure of Ukranian bells

Across the sky one Sunday in the month.
Worn as a saltblock its history tells
Of the steppes' fugitive congregations,

Their immigrant music. I shut the gate
On a graveyard where nobody mourns,
The cairns of infants and fissured angels

Surrounded by the white miles of the wheat.
Those prairies are a stubblefield of nations
Now invisible. And as we left,

The Harleys all took off towards Alvena,
Its beverage room and the Stones' jackhammer beat.
We had lessons in anthropology

That afternoon, a group of us, teacher,
Geologist and myself, looking
For relics of what never made it through.

Our driver dosed himself with three
Different medicines: depression, asthma
And something to which he never confessed.

So I turned on the Byrds' nasal guitar
To keep him awake, Roger McGuinn
Twelve-stringing 'Bells of Rhymney' as we ploughed west

From Humboldt, a disappearing view
Of the Manhattan Dancehall, that filmset
From the 'thirties, a saltworks where the cowl

Of a Buick painted the alkaline thorn,
And from sweatlodge to the Sundown drive-in
Took less than the sixty-minute cassette.

Living culture can also be forlorn.
There was that bad day at The Senator when
The Indian couldn't pay for his pitchers

Or the lined up shots of Tennessee mash.
I watched that tipsy Cree, with his pony-
Tail and rodeo boots, scrounging quarters

In the men's, and remembered Vivian,
Who hid a fortune in a biscuit tin
Under the floorboards, parcels of dingy

Fivers wrinkled like toffee papers,
The golden rashers of the 'fifties –
Three thousand, three hundred and thirty-seven pounds

In a sad-eyed pornographic stash.
His sound was the spokespin of a freewheel
Back from town, and in the plastic shopping bag

Always the litre of cheapest cola,
The packet of Rizlas for a thin-lipped drag.
I met him once balancing a branch

From the plantation on his handlebars,
Food for the Rayburn that never went out.
'Dead wood,' he said, caressing the cargo

With a bloodied hand. 'No sparks, see. No sparks.'
Like that black star on The Senator sign
Where the neon doesn't work. And a man says,

'It's a pity but after one hundred years
They're still looking at us for charity.
Might get frostbite out there on the welfare line.

'If it was up to me they'd never have the choice.
Best place for that punk is back on the Rez.'
Yet it was in that bar's long happy hour

I heard the legend of Almighty Voice.
He was a chief they locked in the latrine
For killing a calf. He broke down the door

And ran into the dogwood around the slough:
And the forest swallowed him soundlessly.
There he became the bark of the raven,

The chickadee's reed, a presence unseen
For three seasons, until the militiamen
Found a bed fashioned from scalpings of moss,

A broken honeycomb. High on his ridge,
Almighty Voice saw the soldiers cross
The river, felt the field–gun excavate

A mineshaft in the birch. And now, in Duck Lake,
There is a thirty foot memorial
Opposite the billiards–and–barber shop

With the details of the chief's last stand,
Whilst schoolgirls of the tribe investigate
The video–rack, comb each other's hair,

And the drivers down on Main Street have to stop
For an Indian that tourists understand.
All right, I know, I'm quoting local lore,

Mere hearsay. The details you asked for
Concern my business here. So what about
This small nightmare? It's now a fortnight since

I sat as guest of honour in that church.
Politeness emphasised I was alone:
Poetry has died in similar places,

So the trick is to be brief and never flinch.
On the lectern was a bible like a kerbstone
(Who was it said my speech would be a cinch?)

And then thirty pale Mennonite faces
Looked up over their plates. The reading
Followed dessert. In the basement I could hear

The silver trunk of the furnace judder
Under the floor. From thousand–island
To the bowl of raspberry Jell-o

Our dinner was complete. I was slow to rise
And when I spoke, each word owned a halo
Of silence, huge and inappropriate.

I listened to a voice that came like pleading
And did not meet another pair of eyes.
The man who was paid to communicate

Revealed a world impossible to share.
How hard, I thought, for us to love each other,
As we finished coffee, hung our heads in prayer.

Okay? I think about this during TV
Commercials; sometimes believe I'm living one.
But don't tell me you've not had these fears:

It's that life should somehow be more intricate:
I can't wait around for the next ten years
And the Five Hundred Channel Universe.

My friends here are becalmed in gentle careers
And suffer a cheerful librarianship
Of the soul. We tour the latest roasteries,

Watch the hottest of the new wave directors
With the Friends of the Broadway Theatre,
Frug to bluesmen up from Minneapolis,

But I know what they're thinking as we sip
Our iced Labatts. Now we're all in our forties,
Things are not going to get any better than this.

Or perhaps it's me that's warping out of true.
Take last night. We stomped down the snow that hid
The bermuda grass, fired the barbecue,

And then watched those who love the white outdoors
Grill pickerel, pulled silver through a yard
Of ice, daub it with Miracle Whip, and spit

Bones like cactus pins. In my part of the fish
Was the spine, milky as a dandelion
Stem. There was a girl in folksinger's weave

Sipping a tube of low-cal, a cluster
Of librarians in stretchpants. And the thin
Irony was that all I could picture

Was the glass hexagon of my table
Spread with atlases, maps of the province,
And the turret of one million words

Built with care, the proof of my existence.
Perhaps it could be middle age, I thought,
Measuring the politest interval

Between saying that I had to leave
And leaving. But that table was my own
Frozen lake, ciphered with shadows. Within

Its element I might surface or drown.
Now Carrie retunes to CKOM
Which is twenty four hours straight Demerol:

Donna Summer, The Kinks, Roy Orbison,
Some of the Lennon tracks from *Rubber Soul*.
It's like the methadone for loneliness.

Outside, the strip is abandoned until dawn.
Here, midnight starts at 6 p.m. and when
The change came it was sudden, merciless,

So that Fall now seems deceitful. We had blazed
Down 8 Street without shirts; barelegged girls
On cycles leaving scarves of perfume

And tawny sweat upon the air. But breathe
It now. In the dark the cold is coming
Like a wolverine out of the north.

Celebrity-haired weathergirls advise
On wind–chill factor, the lakes are triple glazed
Where fishermen work with roadcrews' drills,

Their soft-tyred Cherokees trembling above
The cinematic twilight of the ice.
But please don't think that I'm a fixture here.

One month I made Banff, and that first night,
After spinach and the California rice,
I put my dinnerplate back on the rack

And walked down Grizzly Street where the day's snow
Soaked over my insteps. Below, the black
Seeds of a stream escaped the tightening frost

Which swelled like pincushions on each broken tree.
Up at the Arts Centre, a committee
Of women poets was discussing

Another complaint about *sexual looking*,
But suddenly I was down inside a white
Asylum, where the moose-rubbed pines died

Needle by needle, and a spilling
Artery of meltwater scittered free.
A Grand Am filled with laughing Japanese

Kitted out in Timberlands and London Fogs
Asked directions to the Banff Springs Catacombs.
I showed them my vocabulary of shrugs

But really should have squeezed in for a ride
And gone back to my overheated rooms.
Yet I wanted to breathe the mile-high air

That sticks the nostrils together, leaves you
As woozy as a slingshot of Clan Dew.
Perhaps the only thing it cannot freeze

Is the imagination, irascible
As mercury, the madness I can't share,
An image-world that modern life assumes

Is meaningless. Then all around, the peaks
And their conglomerations of shadows
Had grown invisible. Yet they rose there

Beyond the reckoning of sound and sight
In a black horizon beneath starlight,
Shaped by the mind in their immense repose.

Later, in the bath, I towelled the mist
From the mirror and found I did exist,
Placed the dagger of my doorkey on the front desk

And watched a movie in an empty theatre.
So yes, I'm getting out – if the snow allows.
Last week, I think, we found ourselves up near

St Louis, that type of place where the men
Spend all of daylight in the tractor seat
And women embroider stories of farm life –

Cornflowers drying in the porch, a velvet
Elvis on the wall, and then the children
Home excited off the yellow schoolbus,

Telling how they had seen a diamond
Of bald eagles on late migration south,
Which is always a sign of cold weather,

And tomorrow can they go for chicken
McNuggets in PA? It's over those
Great spaces some have claimed that aliens fly

In glowing dishes – not meteors like
The Perseaids – but spacecraft powered by
Unknown energies. Me? I hear what's said

And do not judge. But certainly the night
Out there is a terrifying continent
When summer lightning strides across the sky

Or dust turns sunset green as malachite.
I've watched a clutch of television shows
Where people talk of alien abduction,

The silent figures that raised them out of bed
Like medieval angels born of light.
In the St Louis Hotel those stories

Start in jug-for-a-buck deals most Thursdays,
Norman Greenbaum on the juke, and the white
Flashing around the midnight blue pool baize.

Later, in the back seat of the Lincoln
I closed my eyes on all the distances.
The tape we chose was a mass by Bruckner,

A homage to a god sinisterly
Triumphant. Outside, the shingled barns
Collapsed into stubble of beet and canola

As the choirs reached their eerie ecstasy.
That was music for a big sky touched with
Fire, yet out there in the wilderness

Was a 'no trespassing' sign and some old
Sourdough in a plaid workshirt, waving
Us on from the Hudson Bay trading post.

He said that visiting season was over
And watched us up the dirt track in reverse.
That road led to Fish Creek and we played lost

And found all afternoon, the windshield scrolled
With stinkweed dust. But I was gone already,
I was done with it, finished with all

The roadkill blues. And as the Lincoln rolled
On through the evening I began to see
Part of the bigger picture. Our history.

This continent is whatever I think:
All the Pretty Horses, *Music from Big Pink*,
Yet there is nothing that feels so lonesome

As its first sound: breath of the locomotive
At 4 a.m. across the Great Plains dark
When the hoarfrost hangs blue under the moon

And the northern lights are a dimmed performance
Of the memory, and it is still too soon
For the sun-dogs. For how they learned to live

In these places, Scot and Ukranian
And the frightened Hutterite, secretive
As the lynx, is my answerless question.

But though I come here like a fugitive
It's a place that will mean what I want it to mean:
Appalachian harp or *Sister Morphine*.

There are those who seek the entire show –
Paris, Texas; Paris, Ontario;
But I can step thankful on to the flight home

And know it is here, another family,
Weird and compulsive, and one that grows
Younger each year, and larger, and more perverse

Than Dublin or London or Rhondda or Rome,
Dealing the world its blessing and its curse:
For what it is is what we all become.

She Drove a 'Seventies Plymouth

She drove a 'seventies Plymouth,
Great barge of a thing –
Chrome erosion, filler in the wing,
Rust like a sour tooth.

It was thirty below
And on Second all the stopped traffic
Was throttling out goosefeather exhaust
Thicker than the snow.

But I had to stop dead
On the sidewalk, new workboots
Rubbing a heel. And what do you know
If I'm not staring straight into that automobile

At this native woman, hair
A black fan under her tuke
And every fingernail painted red.
Or something I prefer. Magenta.

I eased the fit and watched her
Take out a white pencil of salve
And moisten her top lip with the care
Of a little girl colouring in.

Then the same with the bottom
Lip. Then all around in a bright
O. I could taste it myself,
That ointment. Sweet jism.

She saw me in the mirror.
I was one yard away with the tongue
Out of my boot. So what are eyes for?
I'm asking. There's nothing I done wrong.

Neolithic

For an hour I watch the sea
                tear itself apart
then go back by the ridge,
gold dust on it, carrion on it,
a tower of fallen sentinels.

            And honest to God
  I swear, though already in a moment
memory will reinvent itself like duneland fire
    suddenly
            she is there
grain by grain forming before my eyes,

Her skin and hair, the pinched face
    and the tattoos as small as insect bites
    and a little feathered purse that might carry her Samsung
    and the child with her
dark skinned, waving a gull's wing
and the sand a spinning tube, a helix –
little twister that writhes into a child.

    Then last of all the man, a head taller –
a stick and a pouch with yarrow in it for their wounds
  – a magician we would call him –
on the dune where the sand blows around in little ecstasies,
but the grains move again

And their bodies
                    dislocate
               and blur
          and the family falls apart
into the stone that smells of sulphur
and into the corals they go, into the orchid
mouths, into the grass with blades
     pale as wishbones
into the umbilicus of sand the lugworm leaves –
 three genies back into the bottle
of the bronze age, three faces disappearing
               shocked
          as the burnet-rose,
               blackeyed.

Don't go, blackeyes, not a handful of sand remaining;
          not a grain.
                    Don't go.
Must my gentle breath destroy you?
But in the ghost-train the siren is sounding
and the skeletons are shiggling on their wires
and now there is no one left but the jetski boy
carving the symbol for infinity
          white across the bay.

After the Hurricane

Tainted love
Goes the voice in the fairground song.
    Tainted love.

*

I watched the sea last night –
    its splintering pavilions –
And walk this evening
    counting broken roofs
To where they lie
A million years unseen –
The storm's gizzard stones:
        volleys of phosphors
        that rained on this peninsula
        and smoke in every gutter's tributary of glass.

On the esp the gale's inventory:
        adzehead of Bethesda slate,
The pipit in his stripes;
And where the anglers might have stood
        a dogfish
Bloody as a tampon.

In the splashzone I count one hundred shoes
But cannot make a pair

And between my feet
The smooth artemis;
500 mls. of Piz Buin.
        Tainted love
Sings the voice in the house of wax,
    And that's not really
    That's not really
    That's not really

*

64

Rikki Dupree
Has deconstructed himself.
Now all that's left
Are a silver pouch
And a bodystocking.

A woman in the audience moves her teeth
like the trick a snake makes with its jaw.

Downstairs, the landlord of The Buccaneer
Crosses monumental arms.
A Norman knight in Adidas training vest
He ignores the phone that rings along the bar
And considers his open door.

Sand is what possesses him,
Every grain a battering-ram,
The thin, gold mercenary
That the wind smuggles in,
Mooching around his tavern porch,

Scene-stealer
And chief dissembler of these parts,
Cutting up the text of what he knows.
It lies quiet now but he can see it breathe.
Bright urchin who has followed him home.

*

They wander past, then back
And past again,
Unable to help themselves.
For there she is –
Under the blue
Horseshoe of the insect–o–cutor
Aphrodite waits in her chemise.

*

Eyes down,
Ladies and gentlemen.
Eyes down if you please.

*

Carved on the pulpit at St John's
Christ is a fine-boned tourist
Roughed up in a ghetto.
        His scourgers are the fairground boys
        who work the centrifuge
        of the Megablitz.
Tonight they'll all be at the Buck,
Boots like cudgels, ultra-violet shirts,
And that's not really
That's not really
That's not really

*

We tie our children to a wheel
And watch gravity
Torment their faces,
Every new exultancy
Making strangers of them.
Look, who is that above the town,
Flying, flying…

*

        Ah Madam X
        Under your ciborium
        What would we have you place in our palms?

*

On their screens a nest of watchmen
Follows this intruder

Over impossible flux,
The blue light of the steel-police Land Rover

A resurrection amidst sea-holly
Burnt white.

*

We stand in line with sugar chins
Waiting for the torturer,

Whilst deep in the finials of the dunes
Kenfig lies in reverie.

A tribe lives there now
Under the traffic, fierce as martens.

They write their texts
On the megaliths of the motorway:

> *Pray to the Masta:*
> *Praze him.*

There were merchants once
Who dealt in rock pool silks,

Slaves who broke their hands
Raising the tall ashlar.

Yet none of them could halt the drift.
The sky descended like a feversheet.

*

The storm has left a cylinder, man–high:
   the maw of a Nautilus
      on a deserted beach
         Facing the sunset.

*

   Tainted love
Sings the voice gone out with the tide.
     Tainted love.

Jack Kerouac Park

You never left.
   As if you ever could.
Mama's boy and broken football star
I find you passed out cold on the kitchen floor
In bourbon's dream of extinction,
   And in the taverns of Pawtucket
And along the walkways by the granite canals
That the Irish built,
Slouching at dawn away from The Acre,
   And here perhaps especially
On the bridges where you learned to fly
On scrawny wings above the Merrimac,
Looking down millstacks
And caressing the broken glass in the snow
On tenement roofs.
   So in your hometown
   I take these photographs.

*

Over in the vinyl barn
Rots the music you helped spawn.

Positively Fourth Street warped and white,
And *Disraeli Gears*' dark triumvirate

Of boredom, melancholy and menace
In diminished leaps across the distances.

Predictably time has not been kind;
But impossible to leave these things behind:

The Piper at the Gates of Dawn
Is obese, psychotic and forlorn,

But nothing sadder than Joplin,
The voice that heroin

Squeezed into a black hole.
Seek her in that demi-monde between Blues and Soul.

Going out of town
I leave
            a road split by frostheave
To listen for bears.
But there is only my own breath
Returning to meet me down the quiet trail.

And those photographs?
  Here's one I took earlier
Of someone you might have liked.
A Jersey girl who showed me the gold stars
On the sidewalk in Christopher Street:
One of them inscribed
            Derek Walcott.
'Dumb,' she said.
            'They think we're pretty dumb
My side of the river.
  All we got
Is Springsteen's cornerboy angst.
The statesong, if you hadn't guessed
  Is *Born to Run.*
But I remember the sand at Cape May
  Like new laundry,
And all the sharp-shinned hawks,
Hundreds of them, down from the north prairies;
  And those towns
That went back to nothing –
The towns that made iron, the towns that made glass –
  All that's left of those towns
To show there were any towns at all
Are flowers that grow where the foundations were.
  And those flowers have names
That you never heard:
  Like *jewelweed*:
  Little saviour in the grass.'

In my room last night
I watched so much TV
My eyes burned, transfixed as an empire
Impatient with what time might say
Induced its own mythologies
And sent them swaggering across the world.
So killing the set
And the coolerator
I went out to the Budapest Hotel –
Chivas Regal in its cabinet
Like a cathedral's bottled bones –
To see the 8 ball shudder around the baize –
That last black I couldn't put down –
Until the barman, hunched in silence,
Sullen arbiter
Of chance
mischance
And all that is possible
Picked up the cue and wiped the table clean.

*

I saw the the maples rising straight as smoke
And birches, black and bridal
Stripped in their nunnery,
While in my fieldglasses through the trees
Walkers passed routemarker after routemarker
Fuzzy as bears, the blue discs
Of the trail they had taken
Or the trail that had taken them
Leading them home.

*

And now
As the polaroid colour
Ripens beside me in the park
I can watch my own ghost materialise
As I seek another ghost
Under the serviceberry on a fine Fall afternoon,
The sun moving down the choruses
Of *Mexico City Blues*,
All the way down the carnelian plinth
Until the marble
is hot as a bakestone
Under your sad sutras.

St Pat's

I stood in the darkness at the last pew
And counted the candles.

Some were as thick as organ pipes, while others blew
Sweet, like chillies in a smokery.

Going in was maybe a mistake
But slowly the faces began to form

Into a window of white and yellow light
Filled with a mosaic

Of the brave and the beaten and the long gone down.
Perhaps it was a prayer,

(How close that sounds to an apology)
But what else was I doing there,

Worrying at the memory of an underground train
With passengers careless of destiny

As if it was a station they would see again
Like Rockaway or Lexington or Euclid Avenue?

Then in the draught along the nave
The candleflames gave their Mexican wave

And the smoke rose pigeon-breasted to the roof.
Listen. Sometimes there creeps up to you

An image whose shape is slippery as tallow,
An idea that adopts you and will not let go.

Within their bowls the flames were swimming
Blue on the wax and the air dimming,

But outside, a man was selling tapers in the street,
The fumes rising around his feet

From out of the subway, a man blue-collared
Like those candles low in each candle cup,

And offering there for a sidewalk dollar
My last chance of holding a candle up.

The Bear

I still don't know whether it was iron
or the idea of iron that brought me there
    but there I stood,
in the arena that shovels had made
as the mounds of slag were swept away
    and the pentagram revealed,
those courses of bricks not even the iron-men had seen
    who had lost their fingertips,
    lost their hair to the furnace,
the furnace floor laid out as a star
where the dew of iron had darkened a century before.

    And there within the pit
    where it had fallen through
lay the red bear of iron,
    iron itself
and the idea of iron fused as one,
stone within it, and veins of uneaten haematite
and dust of boys who had served the fire,
the bear uncovered at last,
    a ruby under the earth,
but more like a god I'd say
whose priests were dead, and here was daylight
for the first time in that pit,
the first light ever on the god's bones,
his frozen engineering, his unequivocal eye.

    And we raised our helmets
and the glasses that were filled with iron-red wine
    and toasted the earth
and the god who lay revealed in the pit,
the face of him half-risen, the belly of him half-risen,
and half-concealed, that secret part of him
that still lay within the star.

Then the old men with us at the ceremony
laid out words that none of us had heard –
    like photographs from their wallets,
    dead children sprung to life,
an iron language extinct in grass
but sparking in the furnace now
where the grass was flayed away,
words that could not live with grass
or the iron-leafed sycamores that had stove the furnace in.

And we made our speeches around the god
    whose skin lay shimmering,
    stroked by children and flashbulbs,
and we said we would build a church about him
or that this god would be a museum creature
    grinning from his hearth
    or dancing on an iron proscenium,
and we tested our feet on the furnace floor,
    balancing our merlot,
and we found that we were not consumed,
and so we stood as new gods around an old god in his lair
while everywhere in that earth lay iron rosaries
and the melted weapons of an insane war.

The Hoopoe of Punta Ala

Before the sun rose I dreamed a hoopoe,
But the hoopoe already walked through the garden
Eating the last night's bread.

I dreamed I dreamed a hoopoe, but its voice
Had already swallowed me, that soft
Voice that whooped through the garden

And swallowed the bread and the last night's wine,
A voice so deep it spoke to me
With the sound of a cloud, a cloud that swallowed

The aloe that raved in its corner
Of the garden, and then swallowed the dust
That billowed in drapes over the pineta.

This hoopoe did not discriminate
Between the bread or the wine or the dust
Or the aloe's thrashing arms,

The aloe that raved like a man
Disappearing into the earth in a corner of the garden.
This hoopoe paid no heed to such things

But swallowed them whole with superlative
Surreptitiousness, this hoopoe that walked
Through my head as I was sleeping in the garden

That the hoopoe had dreamed, my fingers
Still tasting of the bread and the wine,
And the hoopoe making the morning,

This hoopoe shaking itself like a yellow
Duster over the Mediterranean
While I was dreaming in the garden

Of the hoopoe swallowing me, and when I awoke
In the morning I saw the hand on the head
Of the hoopoe was holding up the sun.

Voices from The Museum of the Mother of All Wars

The Doorkeeper

Such a key!
Its lock a labyrinth
Of wards. Not even the daylight
Filters in.
How is it then
That the uranium
Dances through?

The Nurse

All my babies shrunken
Like lemons in a bowl.

The Matchseller

Glance up.
Rigel.
Bellatrix.
Alpheratz.
Lit by a man in rags.

The Cleaner

The Cruise missile
Is constructed from a cardboard packing case.

Standing alone in a dusty room
I cup its muzzle

And remember the riverbank near Karbala
Where I fed figs to a horse.

The Artist

I roll the clay between my palms.
   And look – a miracle.
The child is dancing naked before us.
Now on my brush her blood begins to gleam.

The Philosopher

   Listen. There is one lesson.
  If you would gather dates
Then you must wait beneath the palm.

The Stone Mason

  Before the sun burns my neck
  Arak will dry my throat.
    Blood of Allah!
  One drop,
         two,
  My sweat on the slab.
  One drop, two, and the bottle
    Back under the jalabiyah.

The Beggar

You ask, what is the colour of thirst?
It starts green. And turns gold. And soon, I tell you,
It is redder than the red of the watermelon.

The Engineer

  Come with me down one hundred steps
  To where the pumps are stilled.

  Welcome to the underworld!
  And a lake such as you have never seen before.

  But why turn away?
  Why cover your mouth

  As if you choked on a bone,
  Or stopped yourself from crying out?

The Muezzin

Soldiers who spoke
A terrible language
Broke into the mosque.
Look, here are the words they wrote
In the blood of the boy who serves the priest.
Our translator weeps.

The Taxi Driver

They gave me all I asked
And a Pepsi I will take home for my wife.
But see how, parked two hours under the palms,
The oil squeezes itself into the light.

The Guard

A woman brings me bread and dates.
I give her toilet paper.
So we stand under the green star and listen
To the night's first sirens,
To the muezzin through his microphone.
Then, slowly, faint as reeds in the Tigris,
Starts our own murmuring.

The Nun

They dug in the tombs
And found only lily roots.

Would they peer into the blue mouths of goats
Thinking them gun barrels?

The Teacher

Not a page, not a book, not a crayon.
If there was glass in the window
I would tell my children to breathe a mist
And with their forefingers write what has occurred.

The Curator

You have been the first visitors
For many days

So especially for you
I will open the secret room.

Could you have ever imagined
What lay within?

And thank you, thank you
For the big, grey 250 dinar notes

That you have plucked out like dead flowers.
Or the pages of a burnt book.

A Welshman's Flora

Ivy

They read poems here every year
In memory of the last king,
Ambushed and strung up.
But he was no better than he might have been –
That leather apron over his arse,
An iron lid on his heart.

Carnation

I stayed in Richard Burton's buttonhole
A whole week. He never even changed his underwear.
And always the same formula:
Start with champagne, finish with scotch.
That kind of desperation is what life's all about.
I wouldn't have missed it for the world.

Chickweed

Before you cover me
With your glass parliament
Think of what I might have been:
Silver ratchet of the dew,
Andromeda in the grass.
But not enough, gentlemen, clearly not enough.

Oak

Visions?
I am cursed with them.
Last night I saw
Albert Pierrepoint's rope
Thrown over the pub coat rack,
A man with no face on a burning ship,
A sleeve of ale turned inside out.

Leek

Yes, yes, a field of white
Balloons. But after his stroke
The gardener never came back.
And now we prefer it like this.
Some of us have even opened a book
On who will be the first to float away.

Pansy

Life was so simple then, didn't know I was born,
A well-kept border round a new-mown lawn,
Slug pellets scattered like small sapphire stones,
Then she sews me on her knickers and throws me at Tom Jones.

Saguarao

I was raised in Swansea, up on the Buckskin,
South of the Bill Williams,
And flowered regular every year.
But it's a ghost-town now, the doors
Stove in and the power off.
You could be a genius there
And nobody around to give a damn.

Bluebell

One May dusk a strange thought:
That here under the trees
We were the Silurian army,
With woad faces, hempen caps,
Waiting for the signal to rise.
But in the next moment the wood was fully dark.

Sitka

Deep in the forest
Nothing has stirred
Since sleep made his kingdom
On my golden cushions of rust.

Japanese Knotweed

Mattock, flamegun,
Monsanto's box of rain.
But why the vendetta?
You of all peoples must understand
Some things need to be covered up.

Enchanter's Nightshade

Life's a strange trip:
That's what's been said
From Iolo Morgannwg
To The Grateful Dead.

Sunflower

November the sixth
All you find on Rudry Common
Is a plot of white ash
With a radial's wire wreath at its axis
And my trunk the empty
Barrel of a thunderflash.

Poppy

Take a handful of these black seeds
And scatter them in secret in the trench at Cardiff West.
Soon the names of our heroes will grow scarlet
Around the Granada services.

Rose

Anthony Hopkins was right.
When I look in the mirror
I don't know who I am.
The aliases, the identities
Are like someone else's dream.
I've even thought of going home
But there can't be anyone left by now.

Henbane

With pyx of poison, acid bath,
Torturer and psychopath,
I spend the off-season indoors
In the chamber of horrors.
Or would you rather meet first hand
This quisling of the narrow strand?

Fuschia

Think of the corner of West Bute Street,
Hail tamping down on car roofs,
The women with pushchairs and children in arms,
As red, and red and orange, and orange and blue
Their saris swish above the wet pavement.

Snowdon Lily

No one has described it
But did you ever see the flame in a miner's lamp?
That candle burning late
Is the guttering intellect of slate.
            Ha!
     Now the last one
Is almost in reach.

Thistle

And you thought Brando
Was the wild one.
Last night in Pisgah Street
I broke into a swanky vault
And headbutted an angel.
How I swell beneath the blue pins of my hair.

Clover

Christians magicked me to stone
In the National Museum,
But I recall a girl who lay
Hot upon me half the day,
The foxglove bell that was her fanny,
And her arse a bowl of honey.

Hemlock

This time the mad cows
Are nothing to do with me.

Sea Holly

One by one
I watch them drown,
The men from the lifeboat,
And the sea lays them out
Across inscrutable Sker.
But I hold my ground on this peninsula,
Looking the hurricane
Firmly in the eye.

Celandine

Yellow as sarcasm, they laugh.
This kid's too clever by half.
So here I am, the precocious one,
Waiting for my country to catch on.

Nettle

Small, low down and dangerous.
Ron Davies never noticed me
But I'd lived on Clapham Common all year.
So what I know is what I know. You know?
It's all being done through my agent now.

Coltsfoot

Can you believe it?,
No bigger than a pound coin,
Yet just as breakfast turned to lunch
They decapitated me
On the drive-in forecourt
Under the dragon flag
And golden boughs of McDonalds.

Convolvulus

This is my country.
I have put down more roots
Than InterCableTel or Microsoft.
I am the forest that grows on the forest,
The fog upon the frost.

Daisy

11 a.m. and I'm the first
Of the regulars in at The Buccaneer,
The usual waiting for me in its dewy glass.
But it's more, my friend, than the sacrament of beer.
My life is one long ritual of thirst.

Green Winged Orchid

Sometimes I hear the fairground at night,
All fire and wheels and acid house,
The videos yammering in the caravans,
And it feels as if they're with me here,
The Ripper, Our Shirl and Godzilla
All trampling over the dunes.

Daffodil

Saint Peter's leek?
I want to be cool
Yet people speak
Of a polite child
Embarrassingly dutiful.
It's time I ran wild.

Wayfaring Tree

For the lost souls
I give directions,
Nodding the way
With my crown of zircons.

Magnolia

People flung kale and cobblestones,
But all I did was bring reports
Of the world that is to come.
Now here I lie, here I lie
Under the walls of Segontium,
The colour of old bones.

Grass

The only time I see your eyes
Is when you cut me down to size.
Or count your acres.
Or hide your massacres.

Mistletoe

Is there no one left who cares for what has been?
Once the gods demanded my advice,
I hung like Arcturus on a royal architrave.
Now I toss dice
And watch barbarians strutting over our demesne.
None great? None good? None old? None wise? None brave?
The times are lean.

Mr Multitude

I'm in the thicket:
held fast. But soon I'll ease out of the thorns,
freeing my hair, my sleeves.
Soon with the ocean on my left
I'll walk into the town.

        John,
under its hood the computer waits
and the e-mails are stacking up
and the net widening with every breath.

But there's nothing new, you'd say,
everything a flashback to something else,
      all that acid you dropped at SFU
still flaring, old sites miraculously come to life,
more ghosts than islands in Vancouver Sound,
for hand in hand the dead and the living will walk forever
        through the mind's marriage.

      But now
eight hours adrift
as another dark grows deep
I'm out amidst the midnight dunes
on a path through the blackthorn.

You know this place. Once you stood here
and to your codex added *bryony*,
a recipe for that banquet you were planning
      for all the conspirators
      who had done you down.

      So many poisons.
But the blackthorn is anti-matter, John. A hole in the night.
Here's blackthorn like the afterglow
of some inferno, its smoke behind the eyes.
My Northern Lights, you'd say, but this
      is ancient territory
and I am humble amongst its ghosts.

        Normally
you would be waking to Hendrix
and bathing, for patriotism's sake,
to Bachman-Turner Overdrive
as the prairie begins to construct itself
from graphite, mother of pearl.

Then at 9, nothing is sweeter
than a JSB partita

unless it is Miles blowing blue
all the way through *Bitches Brew*

while with eggs and coffee in the porch
you begin the day's first watch.

Five miles south on Blackstrap Hill
stands Fra Angelico's goodnews angel

helmeted into his halo, wings
tucked into a Dundurn Wheatkings

sweatshirt. At 10, more coffee and a slug
of scotch to dislocate the dialogue

between mind and heart.
But soon the wheatfield heat must start

and the psychotic and erotic in familiar feud
explode around Mr Multitude,

that Scottish-Canadian prairie dude
on a cocktail of Kierkegaard and Qaaludes.

Yeah, philosopher, poet, piper, pseud
I've renamed Mister Multitude:

the decal on whose Plymouth says 'bad attitude'
so get your ass out the way of Mr Multitude:

monkish, drunkish, sublimely rude,
that face in your face is Mr Multitude…

I could go on.
     But right about now, John,
the surgeon cuts into your throat.
And what terrifies is that you lose your voice.
Not life, you write, in the round e-robin
to connected friends, but voice, that two-string fiddle,
and I hear your proclamation from six thousand miles away:

   Take anything you want, doc,
but leave the sound of the words,
not even the words themselves but the sounds they live within,
the heartbeat of language,
you can understand that, doc,
  the rainfall on the tongue,
  that glottal wine-fur
  thick and indigo,
  O doc, like trincadeira
beds down with cabernet sauvignon,
  but local grapes
with a raw Pacific tang, a harvest still
amongst all the extinctions of BC's enslaved coast,
the sound of the words and therefore their taste,
as the tongue in the head grows heavy
and its purple cordage beats.

   So, John, here's
to a steady hand
as the surgeon slices in.

Such a line he draws –
   a horizon to the heart.
And what I see is the black roof of the Cadillac,
   that Fleetwood parked
in the alley in Dundurn, the *for sale* sign
in the window and already
the dogwood's tongues over the fender.

And, John, didn't we drive
like fools over the Hutterite field,
the flume of dust behind us half a mile long,
the wheat cut and the prairie turned to grey and apricot
like the strata of a fallen cliff,
goldenrod still flowering in the irrigation ditch
and the moon rising behind that Mack with one headlight
    out on the crossroads
    by the Exxon sign?

    The deer were drifting
through the aspens between us and the road,
and when that white cyclops hit its whistle
we and those muledeer and every living thing
    spooked the other way.

    So, Mr Multitude,
    where is home?
Blake's London? Some rundown mansion on Parnassus Street?
The prairie too has its masquerade.
    We stood in the frost
as the aurora wrapped itself around the sky
and saw what the radiographer sees:
    a civil war:
    cells multiplying
      and dying
    in light's embryo.

    Not a leaf out yet
but the dark is saturated in flowers,
that blackthorn perfume of sawdust
and allspice, sea-mist in it too, and surely the blackthorn
        smells as ghosts must smell:
        rancid and electric.

        It is ghost-hour here
and there's a swan's wing of blackthorn against my face –
my own blood-scent a part of the perfume
through the mist of a midnight where I stand
motionless, mouth full of blackthorn
        starry as Staropramen,
        its foam flying.

And didn't we drive, John?
Or did we?
In my head we drove,
that stately car our wheatfield limousine,
and as we careened round the wheat's grey lots
its dust poured out of my pen,
and who was that waving behind us
and who was that waving ahead?

Figures
glimpsed
and vanished
that we toasted with our go-cups.
Who were they?
Teenage lovers, or solitaries
walking out to view
the town's fretwork of light?

But what I learned
is that once under the fence
the prairie teems with spirits.
Its world is full, John,
voice upon voice,
the prairie night a honeycomb of souls.

Salutations to all,
to the multitudes we sensed ahead of our headlights
as if they were the wheat newgrown,
tall and murmuring,
the midnight wheat that sighs beyond your porch
in its invisible cities.

We challenged those spectres
with cinnamon tea and such a shot of Ballantine's
        I could feel my mouth
fill with hoarfrost and cuntjuice and keycutter's swarf,
        a mixture for the memory,
and how those stars vibrated on their wires,
Andromeda pulled low as a child's mobile
over the stubble, or a ghost-buggy that loomed
behind the Hutterite barn, its axles all dazzled up,
                and there was Orion
                    tipping like a salt cellar
                  its three
                  eyelets
                   in the night.

                Such swarms.
Our eyes drank until we turned for home
to sprawl before *Fargo's* white farrago
(those Coen Brothers' videos with a whole shelf to themselves)
        and as we slept
the deer in the aspen wood
withdrew their hooves from pockets of silence:
        the deer in the aspen wood
were a shoal that leapt the electric fence,
their eyes a meteor shower falling through the dark:
            while over our heads
            the sky's migratory lightnings
            burned and fell out of the north,
            burned and fell and burned again
            though daybreak could come no closer
            than its appointed time.

The Ghost Orchids of Berdun

Ace of diamonds
three of clubs.
The lorry drivers put down their cards
and swing into their cabs
where the rosaries wait, the photographs
of women with orchids in their hair.

The previous day I had come to a village
where henbane stood in its sackcloth.

On the wall of the tavern were one hammer and one scythe.
On the wall outside was an iron hook.

I had started drinking at dawn
but always the brandy looked down at me
while I never looked down at the brandy glass.
The wound in the barrel
was bleeding black light.

I had walked in the pass
with my book and compass
and without raising my eyes I knew they were there:
the vultures on their rampart.
And what I was to them the grass was to me.
Our eyes had discovered something growing out of the earth.

That day, I had come up from Berdun
with my carton of wine and bread sliced into napkins.
It was a lorry drivers' halt under the pines,
a tap there, a table, a coil of rope, a tarpaulin, a bucket of tar,
and I sat under the pines and made a spout for the wine
and there were others there. Waiting for me. In the pine dust
and needles, those others, waiting in that dust
the pines were shrugging like ghosts out of themselves.

What are you? I asked.
What makes the you in you?
    And I stared.
These ghosts that had given birth to ghosts were the daughters of ghosts.
    I stared.
At three moons in their orbits stilled at my foot.
    I stared.
At three sisters who were dancing barefoot
and the pine needles did not pierce them.
    I listened.
Three ropes were pulled taut in the earth's belfry.
    I listened.
Meanwhile, three messengers had arrived
carrying the golden saddlebags of language.
    I saw.
Three effigies of myself in salt and iron under the pines.
    I heard.
Three strangers reciting backwards my biography.
    I looked.
Into three microscopes that had fixed themselves
    on the one cell of this world.

Maybe three moths, I thought,
in my dungeon of daylight.

Or the plasma that a centrifuge
had beaten from my blood.

Under the earth
the ghost orchids sleep on mirrors.
Their bandoleras are thrown about them,
their horses laden with bread and bullets
and apricots' shrunken meat.

Every year
the ghost orchids
are a revolution
in this manilla dust.

I had started walking at dawn,
and always the vultures looked down at me
while I never looked at the vultures.
I was the traveller in the pass below the snow.

Now here I knelt
at a calculus of orchids under the trees.
But theirs was a closed system,
and these were initiates
deep in their doctrine.

With my ear to the earth I listened to their chant.
With my eye to the earth I saw their energy was blue.
It vectored in their veils.

What are you? I asked again.
I had seen orchids with faces
like cadillacs and pterodactyls,

orchids slow and greenhaired
as sloths, and indistinguishable
from the mosses where they clung.

The lorry drivers threw down their cards
on the floor of pine needles;

they ate the bread, they took the wine,
they darkened their necks under the tap.

Stretching like lurchers
they climbed into the cabs.
How steep the road was ahead
through the empty villages
past the tavern doors where old men used to sit.
And how soon there was nothing left of them
but the dew of their diesel.

What could I do?
I was the only witness.
The one survivor left among the pines.

It was I who stuffed the oilsoaked rags
into the mouths of the ghost orchids:
I who poured the tar
into their transparency.
It was I who hid their graves away
under the tarpaulin.

But it is no use.
There's not a drop of the green world in them.
They root like plutonium
        in the bone,
their seeds are chariots racing around Troy,
        in their minds are more multitudes
        than Microsoft.

Traveller, I can tell you
there is nothing like the orchid's spur
to slash through this world's skin.
And choose for yourself the orchid's eye
to see into the soul.

I stand in the clearing of the pines
where the bodies have come out of the ground.
The corpses point their fingers at the firing squad.
The ghost orchids
                    the ghost
                            orchids
have returned
as every year they must return.

Under the pines
I learn the grief of ghost orchids.
What can I say that our conspiracy permits?
My genes are only a poker hand:
ace of diamonds
three of clubs.
What I make of myself
I make

as the lorry drivers throw down their cards

as a man approaches the snow line

as the wound in the barrel bleeds

as the lorries climb

as the vultures look

as a man puts three wafers of snow to his lips

as every year at this time
in the clearing under the pines
the ghost orchids
the ghost orchids
wait with shovels beside their own graves.

The Porthcawl Preludes

Salt

Pray to the inexhaustible.
Sip the venomous vintages.
The first
            and true
Religion of this world
Is thirst.

The Drowning Man

Over my head
The grey pages
Float down from the photocopier.
How could I ever have doubted
The sea's apocrypha?

Neap

Surfer, cursing the calm,
Oystercatcher beeping like a smoke–alarm,
Anglers weighting their lines:
Now and forever the sea's concubines.

Oyster

Tonight there's no mistake:
Moonlight on the wave
                is a sunken Taj Mahal.
Within me now the ache,
The premonition of the pearl.

Foghorn

I am the call to prayer.
So let us now consider
The sulphurous god of Nausea,
The ivory god of Enervation:
Today's ruling deities of the ocean.

Buoy

Forever voicing melancholy
Let my fate prevent your folly.

Ammonite

Like you I dream of a tropical coast.
Unlike you I see
The prefecture of fern,
The spunkhot churnings of Godanwaland.

Lighthouse

I fly a kite around my head,
A restless, broken thing.
Is no one there who'd let me rest,
And take the silver string?

Razor Shell

Allen Curnow told me this
And it's the best advice you'll ever get:
Never turn your back
On an ocean.

Creel

I prayed for a mermaid,
And, God's truth, in she climbed.
I'd hold her yet in my oubliette,
A voodoo child of Port au Prince,
Black as a cormorant, her eyes
Shining like comb jellies.
But…I awoke, beached…uncrated,
And even the dream is dehydrated.

Rock Pool

Where but this mirror would you find
Forgotten youth, imaginary joys,
The selves your single selfhood left behind,
Those indigo girls and boys?

Metereologist

I watched the sky turn opera black
  Over Misteriosa Bank. And the ocean?
That first wave would have filled a cathedral.
  Because what is science after all
  But prayer with our eyes open.

Dogfish

  I am sprockled
      Like a foxglove,
          My teeth
  A silversmith's hammers.
  Yet, like you, I will be overwhelmed
  By the riptide in the blood.

High Water Mark

  The office junior spilt my tea,
  Is good at office mimicry.
  When I confessed I'd die for her
  She told the girls on the tenth floor.

  In corridors I see their eyes
  Sated with their own surmise.
  When the e-mail comes from Personnel
  I'll tell them all to go to hell.

Iceberg

Here I drift, golden as a mosque
Through the noon heat of Baghdad.
  Dark birds descend upon me
  And on every thoroughfare
Pilgrims stagger backward from my shrine

Jellyfish

I once saw
Your white disc lift from the prairie.
Now here you are again, the moon's
Placenta, washed up on the shore.
  But what is this within you,
Your heart, your brain, or your nuclear core
Small as a saskatoon?

Cardiff Bay

Lobsters in the market tank
Crawl slowly round the sand,
But look, their claws are tied together
With elastic bands.

Scorpion Fish

O my Chinese grandmother,
Would it be so hard to smile?
All the lagoon is your sugar cake.

Driftwood

The wine has gone out of me.
The grain has gone out of me.
The sap with its mosquito cry
Has gone out of me.
And all my petals pressed
Within the book of tides.

Surfer

Fjords? *Cwteri?*
Every isthmus
        A temporary
                Parenthesis?
So much contained by so little.
            Like our own skin.
Marine biology is an apology.
            The sea's within.

Sand

Ah, girl in a red scarf,
Writing your name into geology.
Before I forget you
The continents will come to rest
Like broken butterflies.

The Drowned Man

I drank the sea.
It drove me mad.
But now I know
It was the serum for my dreams.

Nautiloid

Life's a beach
For the *nouveau riche*.
This sea's not what it was.

Basking Shark

There is an ocean on the moon, I'm told.
A blue ocean of dust, aeons old.
Perhaps there are sharks there, basking in the swell.
Yeah. Moonsharks in moondust. Who can tell?

Salmon

Look closer.
That is not the new moon
In the net of Orion.
I leapt too far.

Pearl Fisherman

I stand on Euclid Avenue
Before a thundering train
And dream of the sands of Nicobar
I will never see again.

Coelocanth

You and I –
The ugly sisters.
And who is this between?
Time, of course, the kitchengirl,
Radiant in her rags.

Dolphin

The salt has dried on me.
Soon under my skin the roses will erupt.
  But still I smile, teeth
A bloodied knuckleduster.
Now, like all the rest of you, the sea
  Creeps up to look.

Shell

Once again, the girl in the red scarf.
What shall I whisper
When she raises the northern hemisphere
To her ear?

Coal Miner

Two miles out I lay
Like a holothurian, in a beam
Of its own phosphorescence.
  Or a fossil that would squeeze itself
  Back into the seam.

Starfish

So, golden one.
Do I bow or can we shake hands?

Turnstone

Windscissors! Triangulator!
For the first time mathematics
  Stays in my head.
Think what Pythagoras would have made of you.

Shag

Dark little abbot on your rock,
You will have to preach louder than that.
These days the congregation is a long way out.

Doldrum

The office junior has long legs
Like the girls in catalogues.
Such compliments should have their place
But now I dread her sour face.
  Does mercy move her fingertips
  For an effigy in paperclips?

Blue Whale

I know my fate:
It is loneliness.
I feel it moving
Deep as the Gulf Stream around me.
It makes me great.

Sea Anemones

Meanwhile, at a standpipe
In the fourteenth district of Baghdad
  Three sisters shake the water
  Out of their electric hair.

Message in a Bottle

After a generation on the swell
  You uncork my tiny scrap:
Instead of X upon the map
  Stands your name, indelible.

Bathysphere

With my ruby eye
  I looked into the abyss
And learned that language only lives in light.
So who will make the words for what I saw?

Buccaneer

I sailed on a schooner to Tristan da Cuna,
  Broke an embargo around Santiago,
Pirated spices off the coast of Maroc.
But now I'm more of your stoic than superheroic,
  And prefer The Pier to a Norwegian ria,
Or doing the conger around Tusker Rock.

Wreck

The sea took my handbag
And emptied it over the shore.
What's left now but a tissue, a ticket
On the Jurassic's ballroom floor?

Prawn Crackers & Oyster Sauce

It's dark.
Take off your clothes.
Move into the first wave.
    Just sohh.
Now move into the second wave.
Admire your newfound phosphorescence.
    And listen this last time
To the sea's
        Chinese
            whispers.

Horizon

It shrugs its golden epaulettes;
Daylight's petition is denied.
Are we the ones the shining world forgets
Or are there watchers on that other side?

The Ziggurat

At Babel
We stand at the crater's edge
And see not one brick remains upon another.
    But there in the distance
    is Saddam's palace
    white as an egret perched on the hill,
As below us the river,
    vague,
        circumlocutory,
Heaves itself towards Basra.

    Following us
Are men who search for the worst things in the world.
    They look in tombs, in children's desks,
    under a jackass's tail.
Why not tell them, Nazaar,
That the formula they crave
Is the mottling of a melon skin
In any farmer's field,
That the microchips that hold the truth
Are datestones in a beggar's mouth
    sucked white.

    But you are silent,
Intent on the lenses, the spinning digits
In the camera's windows.
Yet for me the moment is maddened by locusts
Swarming around my head, locusts in a thundercloud
Over the mosque.

                    Strange,
Nazaar, that you never see locusts:
But of course they are only words –
                    English words –
        I thought were devouring
The date pyramids under the palms,
Settling over the earth with their wings
    tented like lammergeyers,
So many wings in the swarm, so many mouths
I thought surely there were not enough leaves,
Not enough grains,
                    not enough space
In all the irrigated lands
To go round.

We had come down Procession Street,
The black lens cap bobbing on its cord
And me with the tripod in its velcroed sleeve,
The griffins above us triumphant on the temple walls,
And you had zoomed in and out of the temple doors
            but said nothing.

        And so, Nazaar,
I think we missed the boy beside the well
Lowering a bucket on a rope,
Drawing the Babel water again and again,
The bucket with the stone in it – that dark little meteorite –
Going back into the earth before rising once more,
The bucket with the scarred lip and the stone in it
And the light splashing out of it
            over the waterboy's fingers.

        He too never spoke.
Was I the only one at the crater's edge
Who was struggling with words?
    Language, you might have shrugged,
    the Sony cartridge purring in your ear,
    is simply one more thing that drives us mad.
    Or gets us killed.

So make the film
And I will hold it in my ribs,
Riding on the breakneck bus through Badiet esh Sham,
The sun behind me rising like the gold breast of the mosque.
                    Make your film
And I will carry it to the border
In a bag of dusty clothes
And wait between the wires while the protocols are read,
                    thinking:
Land-mine?
                    Or nerve gas?
Language is both.
But also the schism of the tongues,
The liar's catechism.

    Ah, friend,
Do you imagine I cannot see
That you never point the lens
Through this thin Euphrates haze
                    to the ziggurat
They are building on that hillside to the north?
The emperor is at home today
And looking down on Babylon he will understand all things.

He is the griffin, Nazaar.
                    He is the camel
That becomes the crocodile,
                    the lion of black granite
That has broken the pilgrim's back.
Every step we take here he permits.

And Nazaar, you never saw me
Walking down Philadelphia Road
With the Welsh alphabet under my arm
– Apple to oxen in a Debenham's bag –
The glass over the poster smeared with rain
And the builders in Philadelphia Mews
Smiling at the bard in his nightshirt,
That white lyre, at a tomcat
Jettisoning musk, and a stag-beetle
Holding up a mirror in its horny hands.

Twenty-eight letters ran down my arm
In a Brythonic tattoo,
My gold tooth aching in the easterly.
        Words are relics, too, you'd say:
            the shrunken hearts of saints in lead bottles.

            Yet Nazaar
There is a word
            you never use
No matter how I prompt
Or make any other answer impossible.

Remember the city we left today.
In every room is a photograph
            you do not see,
On every corner a statue
You pretend was never there.

On its walls our choruses
Of stars were first chanted.
Think how Betelgeuse
        and Bellatrix
Burn through the city's nox:
While the censor dreams below them
        on his stone bed.

    Tonight
    when we return
    keep close to me
    and whisper that word
While the searchlights on El Rashid Street
    write an X upon the sky.

    But this afternoon
We are Babylonian ghosts
And follow the road uphill,
Passing the guards with their British weaponry,
    the road circling until it reaches the summit
    and we walk under the *iwan*
    where twelve Mercedes wait on the gravel
    arranged in a black sundial.

And the view is all.
Behind us it immensifies.
The little sand-jinns dance like children running out of school
And down Procession Street,
The river lies supine under its mist
While along the palmtree colonnade
A man comes bearing a tray.

Take the sweets from him, Nazaar.
                Give them to your quiet sons.
Take the medicines he offers to your daughter
Palsied in her cot:
                and for your wife
Who waits in your room by the marketplace
And who swells once more, golden as figmilk,
Take all the dollars and the dinars and the royal Jordanian pounds
And buy her a bracelet
                of watermelon seeds.

From the Rock Pool

1

One night an arm stretched into my room.
It was the lighthouse beam
scattering a handful of salt.

The next night the hand brought
a child's bones
burning like driftwood with a small white flame.

The third night it set down
my own biography:
thirteen white pages in a white book:

On the first page of that book I wrote:
what could a rock pool ever be
but a bridge that serves the selves?

2

Last week at the airport I met the sea in Terminal 1.
She was drinking Finnish coffee and reading the Dead Sea Scrolls.
On one ankle was a tattoo of Australia
while Greenland was inked in blue over her breast.
This is fate, I said. Do you come here often?
And I stared into the icebergs in her eyes.
Fate, she said, has nothing to do with it.
And if the Welsh could swim
   they'd be Irish.

3

I held the microphone
to the water. And now I can play the sea's voices
at night. At night an old tide
rides next to my ear, its
grand co-ordinates, its inexhaustible
mutterment. But the sea's language
is what the heart translates:
a tango under the cliffs,
Twentieth Century Fox's heraldic chords.
   Here in the rock pool
   I have conducted them all.

4

In the Apollo I was dancing with a woman I had never met before.
But when I brought our drinks back from the bar
the sea was kissing her arm, the sea was touching her hand,
the sea was sliding her fingers over her hair, her long black hair
that smelt of almonds. So what could I do? Tell me, what could I do?
What could any man have done?

5

The concert was terrifying.
All I heard
Was high tide crashing
In the orchestra pit.

Then yesterday
There was a seagull's voice
On the answer-phone.
I think it was a kittiwake.

6

Kneel a moment
    and watch below –
look, there in the undergrowth –
those lacerated lives.
Their eyes and their hands know the deluge
is due.
    But I –
    I know nothing.
I stand in exile
watching my footprints disappear
like breath off the sands.
    Nothing that leads up to me
    has lasted.
There is no baptism here:
there can be no consecration.

There is only what the tide leaves:
    a Sanskrit of coal,
    a McDonald's plastic lid,
    an empty hourglass.
Until the next of times
            and only the next of times
these too have their appointed place.
    But I who was born in the rock pool
  know nothing has lasted.

7

Today the sea is dressed
  as my doctor's receptionist.
You must have an appointment, she says.
Without an appointment there is no one to see.
  If you have no appointment
  If you have no appointment
  If you have no appointment
      you do not exist.

8

Should I wait for wisdom here?
I could write on a napkin
all that the sea has to say.
The sea that knows every atom of herself.

    I made a tape
    of the book of tides.
    I could play it to the concert hall,
    to the computer,
    to the sky,
    yet only the heart
    might translate it.

9

Midnight, I was shopping in Tesco
down the aisle with the starfruit and the figs,
down the aisle with the chimichanga and the burritos,
down the aisle with the black bread and the white bread.
And I could have sworn
I could have sworn
but every time I looked around
there was only an old man, a young woman,
a child with a windmill.
I could have sworn
I could have sworn
but there was only an old woman, a young man,
a windmill turning round.

10

Somehow the sea discovered my mobile number.
When she rang me at work I had to go outside like a smoker
and then pretend it was a call from the surgery.

11

I stayed in my room one hundred years
until I heard a knock on the door.
There stood the sea in torn denim
asking me to come to the cinema.
We watched *The Beach* together
but it doesn't mean we're going out.

12

Who are you? I asked the sea.
Sister of the desert, she said.
The same salt,
the same.

Who are you? I asked again.
Lover of the moon, she said.
The same salt,
the same.

What have you seen? I asked the sea.
An iron sun
inside this world.
An iron sun.

I have seen diamonds
smoke on an anvil,
civilisations slip
through pavement cracks.

Dry as ice I lay
between Europe and America.
Below me the stone breathing,
the stone's breath.

13

Now I know
there is an apocalypse
within the rock pool.

Now I know
there is an apocalypse
within the rose.

14

My doctor held the stethoscope to my heart.
  And heard the surf.
The doctor wrapped my arm in a black armband.
  And felt the tide.
The doctor squeezed my balls with a plastic glove.
  And talked to me of drowning.

Now, every day, the e-mails, the text messages
from C. But who is C?
C is a stalker, C holds a grudge,
C has mistaken me for someone else.
We must meet, writes C.
But who is C?
Soon, says C. I'm coming so very soon.

15

One day I dreamt
  I will turn on the light
and the sea will have flooded the kitchen;
  I will switch on the computer
and the sea will have filled the screen;
  I will go to my bed
and find the waves waiting in their heartbreaking underwear.

16

Sorry, but I have stopped counting the faces
  that swim into this pool.
They wait as if I was an oracle
  but what can I tell them
that they have not already heard
in the whip-weed,
or driftwood's liturgy?
  Listen, everything that will ever be said
  must stand on a pillar of silence.

17

Today, like a *torero*
the sea wears a suit of mirrors,
arsenic and gold in her pockets
and the names of the drowned
in a sequence of sequins
   she has sewn into her sleeves.

18

Yet there is a rhapsody
   within the rock pool.
Look here, vines with their air-grapes,
a harvest of breath in the fresh air vines
and the vineleaves wrapping the surface,
   the pool's sky.

   And the sunset?
Think of the tip of Isaiah's tongue
while far to the south-west
the Gower peninsula
   is a ballet shoe
   with the satin worn away.

   You understand?
I have learned to open my eyes underwater,
I have learned to look where there is no light,
gazing down through the waves in my green goggles
as if I peered at a solar eclipse –
as if the sun had cooled blacker
   than all the blacknesses of the seabed.

19

In the Funland arcade I stood next to the sea.
I lost every coin in my pocket
but the sea kept winning money all afternoon.

Lend me a dollar, a dinar, a shekel, a groat, I asked.
An escudo, a euro, a forint, a florin.
A pound, a peso, a crown, a cruzeiro,

Lend me a Skanderbeg beggar's quindarka,
that I can play this game until the end.
But the sea said nothing. Instead she knelt down
and the money-child ran laughing into her arms.

20

Today the sea is dressed as a bride
   who wears black:
a black train of ashes
follows her down the aisle,
   she holds black flowers
that were picked at midnight on midwinter's night.
   When she kisses me at the altar
her tongue goes deep inside my throat
blackening every word I've ever said.

21

Trust no one on the shore.
Not the gull with its eye
   like a papaya seed,
not the fishermen who come to judge,
quiet as the crowd at the crucifixion.

Instead, we must dare the tide.
We must dare the tide.
No matter if it takes eternity
   we must count the roses
   within the rock pool
   and the rock pools
   within the rose.

22

On millennium eve
we stroll on the sand at Kiribati.
How we love these islands, the sea and I,
   and how we love the language
of the islands and the thirteen letters
of its alphabet.
   Ah, the lucky thirteen.

   Yes, if words are coral,
then languages are islands,
I tell the sea. You have yours
   and I have mine.
But the sea only smiles
and holds my hand tighter
   as we walk together into the sunset.